G000097300

MAXIMS MINIMUS

MAXIMS MINIMUS
Reflections in Microstyle

T. BYRAM KARASU, M.D.

ROWMAN & LITTLEFIELD PUBLISHERS, INC.
Lanham • Boulder • New York • Toronto • Plymouth, UK

Published by Rowman & Littlefield Publishers, Inc.
A wholly owned subsidary of The Rowman & Littlefield Publishing
    Group, Inc.
4501 Forbes Boulevard, Suite 200, Lanham, Maryland 20706
www.rowman.com

10 Thornbury Road, Plymouth PL6 7PP, United Kingdom

Copyright © 2012 by Rowman & Littlefield Publishers, Inc.

All rights reserved. No part of this book may be reproduced in any
form or by any electronic or mechanical means, including information
storage and retrieval systems, without written permission from the
publisher, except by a reviewer who may quote passages in a review.

British Library Cataloguing in Publication Information Available

Library of Congress Cataloging-in-Publication Data
Karasu, Byram T.
  Maxims minimus : reflections in microstyle / T. Byram Karasu.
      p. cm.
    ISBN 978-1-4422-1688-4 (cloth : alk. paper) —
    ISBN 978-1-4422-1690-7 (ebook)
    1. Life. I. Title.
  BD431.K273 2012
  128—dc23   2012003568

♾™ The paper used in this publication meets the minimum
requirements of American National Standard for Information
Sciences—Permanence of Paper for Printed Library Materials,
ANSI/NISO Z39.48-1992.

Printed in the United States of America

CONTENTS

ACKNOWLEDGMENTS

Gratitude Is Akin To Love

ROWMAN & LITTLEFIELD PUBLISHERS, INC.

Jonathan Sisk
Senior Executive Editor

Elaine McGarraugh
Production Editor

Darcy Evans
Assistant Editor, Acquisitions

Andrea Reider
Typesetter & Text Designer

MY PERSONAL STAFF

Hilda L. Cuesta
Josephine Costa

MY WIFE

Sylvia R. Karasu, M.D.
L'idée *& Literary Editor*

INTRODUCTION
Philosophy in Microstyle

". . . Short sayings drawn from long experiences."
—Cervantes[1]

Like a poet, a psychiatrist dares to be just so clear, and no clearer. Whenever my students or patients or members of the media have consulted me, I offer them some pithy wisdoms that may be a little provocatively vague. In that sense, our microstyle writing[2]—"Twitter Age" suits me well, since I find that anything that cannot be said in 140 characters—(or 140 seconds)—is not particularly worth saying.

The book features my reflections about loving, working, dying and about everything else—my philosophy about life expressed in microstyle. Most of these deliberations are original. Some are restated from my previously published works, and a few have come from other authors and been reframed by me. Though I cannot acknowledge all of my literary debts, I am consoled by two American philosophers' writings more than a century apart.

Thomas Jefferson, in his famous letter of 1813 to Isaac McPherson, compared the spread of ideas to the way people light one candle from another: "He who receives an idea from me, receives instruction himself without lessening mine; as he who lites [*sic*] his taper at mine, receives light without darkening me."[3]

Susanne K. Langer, a Harvard professor, writing recently says, ". . . ideas of every thinker stem from all he has read as well as all he has heard and seen, and if consequently little of his material is really original, that only lends his doctrines the continuity of an old intellectual heritage."[4] The content of this book, therefore, reflects our collective knowledge and wisdom.

Fittingly, I will finish my short introduction with a micromessage: If you find yourself puzzled by what I have conveyed here, it is because you already knew all this.

NOTES

1. Jarvis, Charles, trans., Riley, E.C ., ed. 1998. *Miguel de Cervantes Saavedra, Don Quixote de la Mancha*. Oxford: Oxford University Press, p. 907, *Questia*, Web, 26 July 2011.

2. Johnson, Christopher. 2011. *Microstyle: The Art of Writing Little*. New York: W. W. Norton & Company.

3. Lipscomb, Andrew A., and Bergh, Albert Ellery, eds. *The Writings of Thomas Jefferson* (Vol. 3, Article 1, Sec. 8, Clause 8, Document 12), 20 vols. Washington: Thomas Jefferson Memorial Association, 1905.

4. Langer, Susanne K. 1942/1979. *Philosophy in a New Key: A Study in the Symbolism of Reason, Rite, and Art*. Third edition. Cambridge, Mass.: Harvard University Press, p. xv.

SELF
From Nowhere to Here

A person's highest psychological priority is "to gain a coherent state of mind"[1]—to be relatively "well-glued." This coherence is a spectrum. That is to say, there is no such thing as "normal." We all suffer from a garden variety of neuroses. Similarly, "abnormality" is defined by the manifestations of a person's "unglued mind," or having the predisposition to become unglued under certain conditions—good or bad.

Stability of the mind, however, does not have an end product. It can always be further crystallized and refined. Or, as frequently occurs, we allow the mind to unfold into itself, and bring ourselves into a subjective impasse.

The normal doesn't mean you.

+↜+↜+

There are no psychological supermodels.

+↜+↜+

The narcissist nourishes himself by self-reference.

+↜+↜+

If you failed in adulthood, by the age of forty, you are running above average.

+↜+↜+

Don't let your doubts rule your life, but make sure that they temper it.

+↜+↜+

If you choose the well-beaten path, you'll be safe; if you choose the less-beaten path, you'll be interesting.

+↜+↜+

If you fear your neediness, you'll settle for less.

+↜+↜+

Yes, cry and laugh, yell, but not too much; "emotional incontinence" is odorous.

+✑+✑+

Ambivalence paralyzes the guilty.

+✑+✑+

Conscience is something that tames instincts.

+✑+✑+

To use sincerity as a technique is the ultimate insincerity.

+✑+✑+

The survival instinct is the source of ultimate self-discipline.

+✑+✑+

Mind transcends what can be measured—therefore, it has no norm.

+✑+✑+

Ambivalence about being worthy of one's ambition is the source of duplicity.

+✑+✑+

Complacency of self is a source of failure in maturation.

+✑+✑+

You are not the only one; "deep down everyone is quite superficial."[2]

+‍✄+‍✄+

Pretending to be real is worse than being false.

+‍✄+‍✄+

One feels better by feeling worse.

+‍✄+‍✄+

Pace of neurotics: Each person has a unique, subjective timetable for growth.

+‍✄+‍✄+

Few get tired of self-understanding.

+‍✄+‍✄+

The only failure in life is "the failure of personal growth."

+‍✄+‍✄+

Adulthood is verbal and emotional self-continence.

+‍✄+‍✄+

The principles of mind are the same.

+‍✄+‍✄+

The essentials of our unconscious are collective: they allow only minor variations for each individual.

✦✦

Every mind has its own predetermined framework—its bias.

✦✦

"Wizards of Id" lack phylogenetic self-knowledge.

✦✦

We all live in our own unarticulatable psychological bubble.

✦✦

Microanalyses of the mind bring subjective impasses.

✦✦

Experience is the prisoner of language.

✦✦

"To hatch from the blissful mother-infant state"[3] is the first step to adulthood.

✦✦

While growing up, don't neglect growing down. You are as tall and strong as your roots.

꘎꘎꘎

The "self" that you find at the mountain top is "the same self you took up there."[4]

꘎꘎꘎

The human dilemma is both unique and universal.

꘎꘎꘎

The only safe transparency is self-transparency.

꘎꘎꘎

The mind best organizes itself not around its visible disorder, but around its invisible order, relying not on what is there, but on what is not there.

꘎꘎꘎

Behind the question, "What do I want?" is the larger question, "Who am I?"—or even, "Am I?"

꘎꘎꘎

You can look forward with joy if your look backward offers no shame or guilt.

꘎꘎꘎

Night dreams and daydreams are "Janus-faced"; they are fallacious but also telling. They may be attempts at finding solutions to conflicts in one's present or past, or rehearsals of anticipated ones.

+~+ +~+

"Psychology makes us something less."[5]

+~+ +~+

Man cannot understand matters beyond the enclosure of his mind.

+~+ +~+

Everyone's life story is wrapped in some romantic camouflage.

+~+ +~+

If your impulse is to punish others for minor wrongdoings, you are probably guilty of worse.

+~+ +~+

Your personal history is human history.

+~+ +~+

Our impulses are an abridged edition of our characters.

+~+ +~+

Do not expect to be loved or admired; just try to be worthy of love and admiration.

+~+ +~+

If you were not attractive at eighteen, not powerful at forty, nor wealthy at fifty, try to be wise at sixty.

۰۲+۰۲+

Don't tell more than you know: it is a sign of intellect going to seed.

۰۲+۰۲+

An adult is someone whose mind monitors itself.

۰۲+۰۲+

Once you get to know yourself, everyone will be revealed to you.

۰۲+۰۲+

Don't feel bad about changing your mind; some minds grow by changing.

۰۲+۰۲+

Man never expresses anything but himself.

۰۲+۰۲+

Self-deception is the quicksand of the mind.

۰۲+۰۲+

Dreams aren't unconscious lies or truths, although they may evoke conscious associations about one's lies or truths.

+∼+ +∼+

Discordance is a natural state from which you need to ring out your own concordance.

+∼+ +∼+

You want to help someone else? First put your own act together.

+∼+ +∼+

Self-love is deaf, blind, free from competition, and forever.

+∼+ +∼+

Only sublimation of childhood aspirations is fulfilling, not the aspirations themselves.

+∼+ +∼+

Don't apologize before you are accused.

+∼+ +∼+

You are what you think. The self, thus conceived by the mind, is potentially reducible to a series of thoughts.

+∼+ +∼+

Knowing means losing innocence.

+∼+ +∼+

Character is a by-product of life long conduct.

٭٢٭ ٭٢٭

Man never finishes growing up; one day he just abandons it.

٭٢٭ ٭٢٭

Despite all psychology and all philosophy, "human beings are still incomprehensible."[6]

NOTES

1. Kohut, Heinz, M.D., personal communication.

2. Nemiah, John, M.D., personal communication.

3. Greenson, Ralph, M.D., personal communication.

4. Gyatso, Tenzin, His Holiness the 14th Dalai Lama, personal communication.

5. Schafer, Roy, PhD., personal communication.

6. Lacan, Jacques, personal communication.

FRIENDSHIPS/ RELATIONSHIPS
Embracing Imperfect Offerings

Though the self is formed within, it is cultivated through relationships. Relationships are the *human echo* that provides mutual validation of ourselves and opportunities for physical and emotional intimacies.

Like good medicine, a relationship can cure or kill you. One of the important components of a relationship is *the dosing* of it. You must take just the right amount of it.

All interpersonal engagements are, in variant degrees, emotionally charged and potentially exhausting. Even the best relationships can overdose a person. The self needs the sanctuary of solitude to sediment. It is equally true that without intimate relationships (real relationships) we are lonely. But the ability to be alone in the presence of another person is the ultimate intimacy.

Do not understand another person too quickly; it is reductive and annoying to the person.

᚛᚜

Optimum vulnerability to a friend is the ingredient of lasting relationships.

᚛᚜

The best relationships are grounded in separation.

᚛᚜

Avoid "neurotic scenarios" with your friends. As to family members, it is already too late.

᚛᚜

Unless you accept people as they are, you'll never get to know them.

᚛᚜

In social settings, everything is material for conversation, and nothing else.

᚛᚜

If you try to be liked by everyone, you'll be disliked by many.

᚛᚜

All relationships are found by cultivation.

+❧+❧+

A helping friend is the one who occasionally gives an unconscious hand to you.

+❧+❧+

No one is really himself.

+❧+❧+

The first task of relating to someone is *affect attunement*, which is like *one note harmonizing*, but silently.

+❧+❧+

All relationships are primarily communicative relationships.

+❧+❧+

Even the best relationships are cumulatingly distressing.

+❧+❧+

Messages are accurately interpreted only by the receiver.

+❧+❧+

Emotional intimacy is the result of mutual unconscious infections.

+❧+❧+

Empathy grows in emotionally intimate relationships, with their crises and adversities.

+✥+ +✥+

An intimate space is where things that cannot be said might be said, where things that cannot be done might be done.

+✥+ +✥+

Fights between unequals eventually become grand equalizers.

+✥+ +✥+

Feeling understood promotes the yearning to understand.

+✥+ +✥+

As long as you divide the world into me and others, you'll be ungrounded in alienation.

+✥+ +✥+

Even metaphorical relationships are not free of conflicts.

+✥+ +✥+

An internal dialogue begins "to germinate in an intersubjective field."[1]

+✥+ +✥+

Only the unconscious can reach the other's unconscious.

+~+ +~+

The person's unleashing of hostility and rage may serve *to vindicate the unloved self.*

+~+ +~+

Never gossip with a friend about a friend; you may lose them both.

+~+ +~+

Too loud to hear: Aggression is an attempt to define the self, not to relate.

+~+ +~+

Close contact without generating anxiety promotes attachment.

+~+ +~+

Separation-individuation is a never-ending process.

+~+ +~+

Silence is like the rest of the language; it is not an inert intermediary between words.

+~+ +~+

If you expand to seek others, you may find yourself.

✦✦✦

Most conflicts are reciprocal misunderstandings.

✦✦✦

Every relationship has its own reality.

✦✦✦

Cultivation of inter-subjectivity is the process of friendship.

✦✦✦

Do you want a healthy relationship? Do not be a chronic rescuer, teacher or moralist.

✦✦✦

Most friends are just better acquaintances.

✦✦✦

Everyone you touch must feel it.

✦✦✦

If it is unseemly, do not offer the truth; but do not lie either.

✦✦✦

An emotionally intimate friendship provides the best solitude.

+∽+ +∽+

A friend as far as the altar is far enough.

+∽+ +∽+

With a friend, just be a friend—not a business partner, a banker, a client, an accountant, a minister, a lover or a therapist.

+∽+ +∽+

Friends are not searched and found; they were never lost.

+∽+ +∽+

If you are not your own best friend, you are your own worst enemy.

+∽+ +∽+

Love may generate anxiety, despair and exaltation; friendship should do none of them.

+∽+ +∽+

Secondary gains undo friendship.

+∽+ +∽+

One at a time—conversation is not a duet.

✦✧✦

Wedding of doubts: Only co-authored truths are real.

✦✧✦

Giving advice is poorly disguised self-promotion.

✦✧✦

Indifference toward a person is a dehumanizing assault.

✦✧✦

Oblivious to life's ephemerality, we eternally fill it with interpersonal dramas.

✦✧✦

Cultivate your inner humor but tame its outer expression.

✦✧✦

Any degrading of others—justified or not—is self-degrading.

✦✧✦

If you treat a person as an object, he/she will become one.

✦✧✦

Let your thoughts run, but not your mouth.

＋～＋ ＋～＋

A good conversation is an interpersonal meditation.

＋～＋ ＋～＋

Every relationship is time-limited.

NOTE

1. Gwathmey, Charles, Paul Rudolph Lecture, Yale University, August 2008.

· III ·

LOVE/SEX
Embedded with Stand-Ins

Only passionate love is associated with sex; affectionate love is asexual. Nevertheless, both demand the same high levels of psychological presence and authenticity, with each requiring different levels of transparency. While full transparency is a requirement for the latter, the former is quickly undone by it.

Sometimes passionate love—"love at first sight"—evolves into an affectionate one—"love at last sight."[1] Regardless of its nature, though, love cannot be faked.

The only currency for love is love.

❧❧

Narcissus fell in love with himself because he felt unloved by others.

❧❧

Homosexuals, heterosexuals—in the long run, all become homo sapiens.

❧❧

Only affectionate love is a human sanctuary.

❧❧

Those who give counterfeit love to the rich end up with counterfeit money.

❧❧

In love relations there are no rules, until you break one.

❧❧

Love not to make yourself whole, but to make yourself loved.

❧❧

Total transparency to your lover invites pity, disgust, sympathy, and anger, but not desire.

✦✦✦

Sex can be a peace ground or battle ground; either way the relation is in need of intervention.

✦✦✦

There can only be one soul mate; if you have more than one, you have none.

✦✦✦

Primitive entrance into a woman's inner space is not lovemaking.

✦✦✦

If you stay with someone without any intention of leaving, you'll end up loving that person.

✦✦✦

Emotional intimacy is the fertile soil in which the soul needs to grow.

✦✦✦

Don't let your mind intrude into your sex life.

✦✦✦

Frenetic activity of a loved one is exhausting; frenetic passivity of a loved one is maddening.

CHAPTER III

+✿+ +✿+

Home is where you are loved.

+✿+ +✿+

You find love where you are found by others.

+✿+ +✿+

Insanity often begins at the heart and then invades the mind.

+✿+ +✿+

Love of the other requires securing the separateness of the other.

+✿+ +✿+

Unless you forget, you'll never forgive the transgressions of your loved ones.

+✿+ +✿+

If you want to change your loved ones, accept them as they are.

+✿+ +✿+

Love transforms passion to compassion.

✦✦✦✦

In lovemaking, don't talk; language preempts the experience.

✦✦✦✦

If you love one person, you may love many.

✦✦✦✦

Infantile love: needs being met are more important than who meets them.

✦✦✦✦

Changes in the relational dynamic between men and women generate confusion, frustration, anger, and rage.

✦✦✦✦

Flirtation has only its own primary agenda; flirtation with a secondary agenda is manipulation.

✦✦✦✦

Erotic Pandora's boxes are not only full of obscene sex but also full of vulgar exploitations.

✦✦✦✦

Adolescence is wasted on priapic preoccupations.

+≈+ +≈+

Lupercalia was torture of women. Valentine was a tortured man, with both false promises and false premises.

+≈+ +≈+

Any uninvited sexual intrusion is rape.

+≈+ +≈+

Love cannot continue with rhetorical interestedness.

+≈+ +≈+

The mind is prestructured to love. Even its seeming hate is a desperate way of seeking love.

+≈+ +≈+

Love is grounding in dialectical ambiguity.

+≈+ +≈+

It is easy not to hear elegant cries of despair.

+≈+ +≈+

Lovers speak in pianissimo; married couples in pianoforte.

+≈+ +≈+

Behind the silence of a loved one is a wish to be understood without verbalizing.

+✥+ +✥+

Love is formative energy.

+✥+ +✥+

With age, enduring love evolves from passion to affection and ultimately, to compassion.

+✥+ +✥+

The inability to love is "the most recalcitrant of all psychopathologies."[2]

+✥+ +✥+

Sexual passion is always in fashion.

+✥+ +✥+

A blush is a sign of being really found.

+✥+ +✥+

All is unfair in love. That's what fuels passion.

+✥+ +✥+

One can't pretend being in love or having the measles.

+✥+ +✥+

There is no school of love; it is an affair of innocent ignorance.

+∾+ +∾+

There are no laws of love. Lovers make them up as they go along.

+∾+ +∾+

The object of love is interchangeable; the feeling one has when in love is constant.

+∾+ +∾+

There is no jealousy in dyadic relationships. Jealousy requires triangulation.

+∾+ +∾+

Jealousy is not grounded in love; it wobbles on insecurity.

+∾+ +∾+

Hatred of the passionately loved one is the most violent type of love.

+∾+ +∾+

The heart has its own eyes, ears, nose and taste buds.

+∾+ +∾+

Passion is sublimated and projected narcissism.

✦✦✦✦

"I hope your heart is in the right place" means it should be in your head.

✦✦✦✦

Dependency, enmeshment, and friendship kill passion.

✦✦✦✦

Fighting couples grow pathologically dependent on each other.

✦✦✦✦

Fear of woman's sexuality is the source of misogyny.

✦✦✦✦

Adolescents need intense same-sex relations—that is not homosexuality.

✦✦✦✦

An infant could have an attitude of waiting to be embraced; an adult must boldly swing into others if he wants to be found.

✦✦✦✦

Empathy and sex are mutually exclusive.

+〜+ +〜+

Passionate love is sex, poetically inflated.

+〜+ +〜+

Love makes itself felt through excesses.

+〜+ +〜+

Passionate love is cured by leaving or marrying.

NOTES

1. Benjamin, Walter W. 1968. *Illuminations: Essays and Reflections*. New York: Schocken Books, pp. 168–69.

2. Cohen, Leonard, personal communication.

IV

MARRIAGE/FAMILY
Winning by Losing

The primary purpose of marriage is to have one's own nuclear family. One may have secondary purposes, i.e., sex, dependency, finances, etc. These secondary agendas are responsible for most of the dissatisfactions in marriages. Some of these lose their importance or begin to weigh too heavily on a compromised self.

This doesn't mean that marriages based on the principle of a desire for a nuclear family are safe from the vagaries of marital life. In fact, the original purpose may become the very source of conflict between spouses once the first "grenade"[1]—a baby—is thrown into the home.

In short, all marriages (yes, there are many types) need steady and deliberate attending to in order to succeed. Independent of our reasons for getting involved with "that stranger," we will have a chance to knit an emotional intimacy with him or her. Yes, it is a job, until it is not.

Why do some quarreling couples stay together? They are suppliers of adrenaline to each other.

✛✛✛✛

Most married couples suffer from some interpersonal symptoms. A trial separation may cure the symptoms, until they get back together again.

✛✛✛✛

A spouse's determination to change the other is negating, dispiriting, and useless.

✛✛✛✛

A primarily sexual marriage leads to mutual objectification and eventual failure.

✛✛✛✛

Men and women need to learn to celebrate their incompatibilities.

✛✛✛✛

Husbands of domineering women are sexual opportunists— "sneaky fuckers."[2]

✛✛✛✛

Don't just tolerate your spouse's quirks; enjoy them.

+≈+ +≈+

Individuation within the marital context is salutary if in tandem; it is dangerous if solo.

+≈+ +≈+

There is no "marriage," but rather "marriages."

+≈+ +≈+

A colicky infant makes spouses scream at each other.

+≈+ +≈+

The father helps the child to separate from the mother and to recover from infantile narcissism.

+≈+ +≈+

Diversify your portfolio of genes: the best gift you can give your children is the genes from another tribe.

+≈+ +≈+

Children need external boundaries to develop their own internal boundaries.

+≈+ +≈+

Adolescent sexuality reawakens dormant sexual conflicts in the parents.

✦✦✦

"The Empress has too many clothes"[3]: the source of common marital arguments.

✦✦✦

It is common to displace personal crises onto one's marriage.

✦✦✦

There is an eroding effect of being chronically exposed to an angry mate.

✦✦✦

The spouse is a life-witness, if nothing else.

✦✦✦

Co-independence is the secret of a healthy relationship between spouses.

✦✦✦

The time-released traumas of marital conflicts manifest in midlife.

✦✦✦

Very few can survive a chronic separate and differentiated state without getting depressed.

✦✧✦✧

Emerging from singlehood or divorce can give one the *psychological bends*.

✦✧✦✧

Irreconcilable differences exist between men and women; they are erotic material.

✦✧✦✧

It is the reconcilable differences that cause most divorces.

✦✧✦✧

To be deprived of a private space—sanctuary—is soul murder.

✦✧✦✧

The *self* is transmitted from parents to children.

✦✧✦✧

Permanency (e.g., reliability, predictability) of parents provides self-constancy in the child.

✦✧✦✧

The question of "whether to marry" should precede "whom to marry."

✦✦✦

It is normal to remain ambivalent about being married and to whom.

✦✦✦

Communicative intimacy is what makes marriages last.

✦✦✦

If you obtain psychological hermaphroditism, you will never need to divorce.

✦✦✦

Monogamy is for the birds, and not even then.

✦✦✦

Marriage may not be for everyone, but emotional intimacy is.

✦✦✦

Adolescents attempt to form their identity by negating their parents.

✦✦✦

The mutual recognition between mother and infant is "the first exalted encounter in life."[4]

Divorces do not occur in a vacuum. Spouses grow apart only when they grow nearer to someone else.

Don't look for faults: the litany of wrongs is inner pollution.

A child needs a maternal woman to become a healthy narcissist.

The catch-22 of mothers; women with infants can do no right.

Men and women exasperate each other by failing empathically.

Protect the solitude of your spouse, not just your own.

Serenity is living a life filled with quiet—with others.

Parents also give psychological birth to their children.

✦✦ ✦✦

Ethics and morality can be internalized and learned only in the formative years.

✦✦ ✦✦

An ability to read between the lies is a skill that every parent of teenagers must acquire.

✦✦ ✦✦

The unguided mind of a child of the wealthy saps itself.

✦✦ ✦✦

Children make parents out of men and women.

✦✦ ✦✦

Teaching, force, or love will not tame youth. Time does.

✦✦ ✦✦

If you don't understand the spousal choices of others, be assured; they don't understand yours either.

✦✦ ✦✦

Like a boat, a person is more stable with two anchors: a job and the family.

✦✦ ✦✦

Marriage is not the wedding.

+⋙+⋙+

Women do not have penis envy, men do; women may have breast envy.

+⋙+⋙+

Highly successful fathers breed sons of Oedipal defeat.

+⋙+⋙+

Marriage vows are not liable for perjury.

NOTES

1. Ephron, Nora. 1983. *Heartburn*. New York: Random House, p. 158.

2. Glantz, Kalman, and Pearce, John K. 1990. *Exiles from Eden: Psychotherapy from an Evolutionary Perspective*. New York: Norton.

3. Karasu, Sylvia R., M.D., personal communication.

4. Arlow, Jacob, M.D., personal communication.

V

WORK/BUSINESS

Transmutation
of the Ordinary

Work is life-literacy, say monks. We learn life by working. Whether we are a clerk or a CEO, we are "bound" by the same basic ethical and moral principles and simple rules of conduct as well as complex formulations related to success or failure.

At the upper echelons of the work hierarchy, "bonds" become tighter and more unforgiving, turning into shackles. An old patient of mine, who was promoted to a top position at his firm, explained his anxiety: "Doc, the higher up the monkey goes the more you see his ass."

Don't fuck down.

+~+~+

Before thinking outside the box, first get into it.

+~+~+

If, like stonemasons of old, you are given the task of *carving the backs of masterpieces*, hammer on.

+~+~+

Energy comes in the doing.

+~+~+

Anything can be interesting if you are interested.

+~+~+

If you think something isn't worth doing, still try to do it well.

+~+~+

You can only delegate to others what you already know how to do.

+~+~+

Interest comes with involvement.

Every expert was a beginner first.

A wise man may err and self-correct; the unwise man remains persistent.

If you are genuinely willing, it is easy; if not, it is not.

Only by avoiding the beginning can you escape the ending.

You may miss your target by aiming high or low, but at least aim at the right target.

To know is to control.

If you aspire to be genius, you'll fail in developing your natural talent.

No one has been able to kill two birds with one stone. At best you'll hit one; unless the other was already dead.

+❧+❧+

Explaining away everybody's mistakes is seeking second-hand redemption.

+❧+❧+

Never bite even if your teeth meet; just show them.

+❧+❧+

In audacity, wishes are promised, fears are conceded.

+❧+❧+

Always recognize your predecessor if you are successful; don't, if you are not.

+❧+❧+

No one can counsel himself well; the mind cannot take enough distance from itself.

+❧+❧+

Self-exaltation is the lack of dignity.

+❧+❧+

He who isn't *battle slain* will *fight again*.

+❧+❧+

Do not drink in public if you have to hide certain traits; with each glass, alcohol will reveal them one by one.

＊✦＊✦

Think of the end and rethink the beginning.

＊✦＊✦

Scientists don't always know the truth.

＊✦＊✦

If you find something to love in your work, you'll feel loved.

＊✦＊✦

No one falls up: you have to forcibly climb; some climb down gracefully, others just fall off.

＊✦＊✦

When you rise, your feet will be washed; when you fall, you'll be trampled underfoot.

＊✦＊✦

If you want to play first fiddle, learn to play second fiddle well.

＊✦＊✦

Talk about the fish that you caught, not the fish that got away.

❧❧

Don't generate busy work; it is better to be idle for a while—at least it has potential.

❧❧

Only after you "dip your bread in your sweat"[1] will you be entitled to take a bath.

❧❧

Avoid self-advertising: it will undermine your own self-confidence.

❧❧

Anything that is worth knowing is known only through experience.

❧❧

Jobs that chronically expose a person to negative stimuli predispose him/her to severe depression.

❧❧

Adaptive pragmatism begins with recognition of the fact that the world is in perpetual flux.

❧❧

You'll feel less alone simply by recognizing that we all have the same emotional stratum.

✦✦

The worthy influence of a good parent is to say to a child: "Go, and try otherwise."[2]

✦✦

The ethics of success is defined by the successful.

✦✦

Success, power and fortune demand sound judgment and even sounder temperament.

✦✦

A boss has to be optimistic and talk of potential successes, especially if he can't deliver them.

✦✦

Do not boast of your honesty, especially if you are honest.

✦✦

The hare was not outrun by the tortoise. They were running two different races.

✦✦

Every job is meaningless if you are not fully engaged in it. The meaning of any activity is a by-product of one's commitment to it.

+⧉+ +⧉+

A boss who seeks secondary gains from his position loses his primary gain: his job.

+⧉+ +⧉+

Solutions to problems are accessed by approximation.

+⧉+ +⧉+

Stating a problem with clarity and without prejudice is half way to finding a solution.

+⧉+ +⧉+

Your motivation will direct your action and will be known.

+⧉+ +⧉+

Fear of failure grows exponentially larger with each success.

+⧉+ +⧉+

Opportunities are not found; they are created.

+⧉+ +⧉+

The art of pretending may be worth cultivating in all professions except in acting.

Too high a "financial IQ" is a correlate of white-collar crimes.

In social communication, the shortest distance between two points may not be a direct line. In business use the direct line.

Energy is fine; aggressive energy is tolerable; transgressive energy is obnoxious.

If your temporary absence is not noticed, it is time to make it permanent.

In professional communication, reduce noise to amplify signals.

Salesmanship means overwhelming potential clients' minds with irrelevant material long enough to close the deal.

It is easier to turn frogs into princes than it is to turn princes into kings.

Capitalism wasn't meant to be looting the planet's capital.

Power is like money: the more you spend the less you'll have.

If your expectations are too high, you'll be disappointed; if your expectations are too low, you'll disappoint.

Relax; no one and nothing can unfailingly tie up all the loose ends.

Some move forward stumbling.

To get back to the surface, one has to hit bottom very hard.

Life evolves with mutability; immutables fail.

Faults of behavior are recognized by the wise and corrected; faults of character are exalted by the unwise and displayed.

⁕⁕

Sitting on the fence too long strains one's buttocks.

⁕⁕

"If you argue long enough about the glass being half empty or half full, the water will evaporate."[3]

⁕⁕

Giving advice is free, but taking advice could be costly.

⁕⁕

Transgressions of silence are underreported.

⁕⁕

The same mind that created the problem can solve it. "The Gordian knot unties itself."[4]

⁕⁕

Success makes your enemies "convertible"; offer them respect, generosity, compliments but never jobs.

⁕⁕

The best substitute for a single success is multiple failures.

✦✦ ✦✦

Do not aspire to play every instrument in the band; be inspired to play one well.

✦✦ ✦✦

Always check the eyes—be they fish, a needle, or a person.

✦✦ ✦✦

Let your brain move your feet, not any other organ; i.e., stomach, penis/vagina, heart.

✦✦ ✦✦

Split the difference when there isn't any.

✦✦ ✦✦

Lend your ears but never your mouth.

✦✦ ✦✦

The sense of infallibility is one's greatest vulnerability.

✦✦ ✦✦

"Do not harm" doesn't mean do nothing.

✦✦ ✦✦

History doesn't repeat itself; we do.

✦✦ ✦✦

Don't nibble at the bait; no fish ever caught a fisherman.

✦✦ ✦✦

Don't hitch your wagon to anyone, if you want to keep it.

✦✦ ✦✦

Failures, more than successes, go to people's heads.

✦✦ ✦✦

The dirt-to-gem ratio in diamond mines is a fair metaphor for life, but not for the diamond dealer.

✦✦ ✦✦

At times "once" is one too many.

✦✦ ✦✦

Opportunity is a psychological momentum.

✦✦ ✦✦

Promise less and deliver more.

NOTES

1. Sufi saying.
2. Fierman, Louis B., personal communication.
3. Karasu, Sylvia R., M.D., personal communication.
4. Hayley, Jay, M.D., personal communication.

· VI ·
CULTURE
Growing Down

Culture is the communal self. Although it is supposed to represent the collective values, tastes and rules of a community, culture tends to get shaped within the quarantine of certain media, television and movies. Therefore, an average individual is, in one form or another, in chronic conflict with his own culture and its creators, i.e., young wardens.

Nevertheless, in spite of ongoing changes, certain intellectual rigor and cultural etiquette remain immutable. One can learn *to be cultured* within a contemporary context and still remain cultured. Like anyone else, those young *wardens of culture* also have, at best, one song to sing. So find a time-tested song, fine tune it and sing its variations.

America is an easy solvent of pedigrees—everyone is his own ancestry.

Necessity is no longer the mother of invention. It is the other way around.

Autobiographies are self-deluding strategies to conceal the truth.

Everything has been said before, but it can be said worse.

"Off-color" misspeaks all languages.

If you know everything and nothing else, don't tell anyone.

What is not worth saying is not worth saying well.

So many words, so little to say.

+≈+ +≈+

Eloquence without wisdom is received with scorn.

+≈+ +≈+

Exaggeration is moral inebriation.

+≈+ +≈+

The more you talk, the more you may lie.

+≈+ +≈+

The less you claim, the less you have to recant.

+≈+ +≈+

One's hearing improves with interest.

+≈+ +≈+

Science issues only interim reports; art issues no reports.

+≈+ +≈+

Humor is cultivated aggression; wit is spontaneous hostility. Both border on insolence.

+≈+ +≈+

Impulsive thinking is an asset; any other impulsivity is liability.

+≈+ +≈+

"Eagles don't flock together."[1]

+≈+ +≈+

Reputation is the external manifestation of one's conscience.

+≈+ +≈+

Philosophy, like any other religion, is largely made up of repolished stories.

+≈+ +≈+

Use calming words even in the fiercest arguments, unless you can totally avoid arguing.

+≈+ +≈+

The artist neither lives nor dies.

+≈+ +≈+

If you know how to give advice, take it.

+≈+ +≈+

Everything you exaggerate loses its real value, no matter how little it is.

Advice always remains rhetorical; it has no impact on the receiver.

Women converse about themselves; men debate about everything else.

There is no such thing as a "free country"; there are freer ones.

Curiosity and inquisitiveness in social contexts are vices.

Only the unreachable sustains our interest.

Walls used to have only ears; now they also have eyes.

Education is intended to form polite, rational, thoughtful and uninteresting people.

+✧+ +✧+

More eyes (I) and fewer ears make a monologue.

+✧+ +✧+

Don't frame your mistakes with trite or witty excuses; they are best fixed with a simple apology.

+✧+ +✧+

Excessive levity and familiarity lower one's respectability.

+✧+ +✧+

A flatterer softens the ears before chewing them.

+✧+ +✧+

Flirtation is the intelligent art of approximation.

+✧+ +✧+

"Unreplicability" is what makes a work art[2]; reproducibility, science.

+✧+ +✧+

The incorrectness of their creative minds is what makes artists so appealing.

+✧+ +✧+

"Pen-envy" is the neurosis of authors.

Art is the communal road to the unconscious.

No gift is ever free; always check the exchange rate.

It is hard to be good; if you cannot be good, try to be interesting. To be bad and tedious is not fair.

Read what you are inclined to read, not to be "well-read."

Don't be too obvious. It is tiresome.

To tell a truth, you need a receiver.

Only the self-promoter's life as a satirist is an art.

Lies and duplicities can only ensure pseudo-cohesion, which, in return, legitimizes being untruthful.

+✦+ +✦+

Most social conversation consists of bad clips from the media.

+✦+ +✦+

There seems to be an almost unbelievable enthusiasm about labeling others.

+✦+ +✦+

"Drivers should stop at red lights" is a law; "Drivers should be people who stop at red lights" is ethics.

+✦+ +✦+

Linguistic quarantine: There is no escape from language.

+✦+ +✦+

Words and thoughts generate systematic misinformation.

+✦+ +✦+

Silence is the edge wherein language fails emotions.

+✦+ +✦+

Arguments have nothing to do with an exchange of reason; they are the abuse of reason.

+✦+ +✦+

Adolescence is to doubt the principles of one's culture.

+❧+❧+

The times will not comply with you; try to comply with them; at worst you'll be called "adaptive."

+❧+❧+

Intellectual discontent is the compelling force for learning.

+❧+❧+

Language is a mediocre translator of thought and a *mistranslator* of emotions.

+❧+❧+

Unfamiliar words are not edgy; they blunt thoughts.

+❧+❧+

Lies told in silence make the loudest noise.

+❧+❧+

Nature is indifferent to our delusional tribalism; it affirms only itself.

+❧+❧+

Computers process information; man distills knowledge from information.

❧ ❧

Frequently checking your Blackberry, Facebook, etc., is informational promiscuity.

❧ ❧

The knowledge that we need resides in the sediment of our experiences.

❧ ❧

Man differs from his real self in differing company.

❧ ❧

Those who praise others too much obliquely praise themselves.

❧ ❧

We all harbor some lies about our past and some lies about ourselves.

❧ ❧

Conversation is not about looking for opportune moments to make self-referential comments.

❧ ❧

The relations between people are not linear, but rather omni-directional.

Do not get into the thick of thin things.

Converse improvisationally. The incorrectness of the running of the bulls is what makes it so appealing.

A theoretical life: A person exists in the discourse of others.

You thought you recognized the person, but all you have done was to engage in a phenomenological reductionism.

Leisure means cultivation of mind and body, at a leisurely pace.

Accepting other cultures as they are is the mark of a civilization.

You cannot just decide to paint, to write, or to play an instrument (and be successful at it); creative activities are inner compulsions.

+♥+♥+

Only absolutes reside in the field of ethics and need no justification.

+♥+♥+

From Pasteur to Dale Carnegie, every wise man praises "thinking" but is never explicit about "what" to think: Undetermined thinking folds on itself, generating obsessive confusion and despair.

+♥+♥+

Literary sterility is an early sign of cultural decay.

+♥+♥+

Man and circumstances alter each other.

+♥+♥+

Life is never tedious; people are.

Notes

1. Szasz, Thomas, M.D., personal communication.
2. Stella, Frank, Metropolitan Museum of Art Lecture, New York City, 2007.

VII

POLITICS
Selfish Saints

Politics is, by and large, a self-serving business pretending to be in the service of people. It attracts the best and the worst but is dominated by the loudest. Over the centuries, some politicians, in collaboration with their counterparts/collaborators in the financial world, have helped metamorphose "The Culture of Narcissism"[1] into the "Culture of Sociopathy."[2]

Yet, even in its most virulent forms, politics has its own veritable truths of survival.

Democracy is a kingdom of the wealthy.

‡≈‡ ‡≈‡

Don't quote yourself unless you want to apologize for it.

‡≈‡ ‡≈‡

If you cannot take comfort in moderation, try to exceed in the good and the high, and fall short on the bad and the low.

‡≈‡ ‡≈‡

The universal rights of people are sustainable only by the adherents of an objective moral code.

‡≈‡ ‡≈‡

In the Middle East: The cast may change, but the play remains faithful to the original script—perpetual conflict.

‡≈‡ ‡≈‡

Only the weak can afford to fight on multiple fronts.

‡≈‡ ‡≈‡

What seems to be insanity in politics is simulated sanity, i.e., a method designed to subdue other insanities.

✦✦ ✦✦

The only way to predict an event is if you are to bring it about.

✦✦ ✦✦

Democracy is saved every four years by regularly occurring pseudo-revolutions called elections.

✦✦ ✦✦

Some cling to the truth in favor, and let go when it is out of favor.

✦✦ ✦✦

Some people offer dreams of hope, while others give only nightmares, but never in the same bed.

✦✦ ✦✦

Politics is like any other business; neither good nor bad, just business.

✦✦ ✦✦

America should only point the way (à la Buddha) to democracy and not try to carry other nations there.

✦✦ ✦✦

Leaderless revolutions fold on themselves.

✦✦✦✦

Naked ambition is stripped bare as Arab nations declare:
Like the emperor of old, our leaders have no thobes.

✦✦✦✦

Revolutions are not reality shows.

✦✦✦✦

The vision of dictators doesn't seem to improve even when
those dictators are backed against the wall.

✦✦✦✦

A nation that fights on multiple fronts becomes vulnerable
to opportunistic aggression from other enemies.

✦✦✦✦

Incendiary rhetoric unleashes violent aggression in unstable individuals.

✦✦✦✦

Dilemma of any leader: *He led his regiment from behind*
and lost many battles. He tried to get in front of his regiment and got badly hurt.

✦✦✦✦

Every politician, regardless of gender, exalts testosterone-fed aggression.

The great leader is a simplifier.

Until they find peace within themselves, nations cannot make peace with their neighbors.

There is nothing irreversible about a mistake, except when the mistake is a political one.

In politics be seen in the middle but never be there.

There is no avenging yourself upon the rich without getting impoverished.

Courage and creativity are dangerous attributes in people who are green in judgment.

Unless you can argue for both sides of the controversy you are a disqualifiable partisan.

✦✦ ✦✦

The polarization of any subject foments hate and paranoia.

✦✦ ✦✦

"We" of timids subordinate to an "I" of any grandiose.

✦✦ ✦✦

If you shadow people with self-references, you'll be in the dark.

✦✦ ✦✦

Even a mature person needs sedimentation time. Drinking, marriage, not before age 18; the presidency not before age 50.

✦✦ ✦✦

If a political speech contains certain internal contradictions, it is designed for hiding morals in the justification of vulgar self-interests.

✦✦ ✦✦

In every form of government money dominates; in autocracy by appropriating money, in democracy by electing the officials.

✦✦ ✦✦

The powerful have an illusion of infallibility that they want everyone else to believe.

No one tells or hears the same story once.

Narcissism is a spectrum trait, and everyone has it; but it becomes pathological when it metamorphs into sociopathy.

All perfections are inauthentic.

Deliberately delaying actions insure not safety, but regrets.

Moral indignation represents the envy of others.

An unprincipled mind tries to understand both sides of a question but remains faithful to its lack of principles.

The wrath of the ruthless is lifelong.

Apologies are recoils, primarily from the potential consequences of bad behavior.

✦✦✦

If you attribute all negative events in your life to fate, that means you have been missing the warning signs.

✦✦✦

The liar believes no one.

✦✦✦

We all harbor some lies about our past, and politicians continue to do so in the present and in the future.

✦✦✦

You are either an authentic being or a plagiarist.

✦✦✦

In *collage* society, compassion (suffering with) declines because there the very *being with* is alienating.

✦✦✦

Abortive variations of speech: Shortening the gestation period changes the delivery.

✦✦✦

Do not reply unless you want to engage further.

If you cannot offer sincere criticism, do not offer insincere compliments.

Deceiving the deceiver is not a righteous act; it is a deception.

If you have enemies in every port, it is time to mothball your boat.

For an individual, reality is perceptual; for a group of individuals, reality is consensual.

No one wants to hear criticism, constructive or not.

Everyone wants praise, love, recognition, compliments, appreciation and admiration, but even more so when not deserving.

Interest in sex scandals is time-limited, as is interest in sex itself. Players must be changed to keep interest alive.

+❦+ +❦+

There are no absolute truths as there are no absolute lies.

+❦+ +❦+

Well-articulated ignorance, no matter how carefully versed, is still ignorance.

+❦+ +❦+

Anger is brief; its consequences are very long.

+❦+ +❦+

If you wear two watches, synchronize them.

+❦+ +❦+

In the melodrama of rights and wrongs there are always unreflective, quarrelsome characters.

+❦+ +❦+

"Reputations, especially bad ones, are hard to live down."[3]

+❦+ +❦+

If you beat about the bush, birds fly away.

+❦+ +❦+

Either row the boat or beat the drum; the idle rock the boat.

+∾+ +∾+

No vice, no virtue is a sociopath's consolation.

+∾+ +∾+

Every secret wrongdoing has its witnesses.

+∾+ +∾+

Don't be embarrassed about changing your opinion; that is the ultimate consistency.

+∾+ +∾+

Most men present themselves as good enough; only hypocrites are very good.

+∾+ +∾+

Neither let anyone hear your secrets, nor hear anyone else's.

+∾+ +∾+

One "trivial" vice will drown all of one's virtues.

+∾+ +∾+

Thinking aloud should be reserved to when alone; in public, thinking should be muted.

+❦+ +❦+

"The narcissist picks his own pocket"[4]; the sociopath picks others' pockets. Politicians do both.

+❦+ +❦+

In politics, facts are meaningful only out of context.

+❦+ +❦+

Most of what we consider knowledge is contemporary information.

+❦+ +❦+

A liar who remembers his lies is a true sociopath.

NOTES

1. Lasch, Christopher, PhD. 1978. *The Culture of Narcissism: American Life in an Age of Diminishing Expectations*. New York: W. W. Norton & Company, Inc.

2. Karasu, T. Byram, M.D., 2011. *Gotham Chronicles: The Culture of Sociopathy*. Lanham Md.: Rowman & Littlefield Publishers, Inc.

3. Buchwald, Art, personal communication.

4. Fromm, Eric, personal communication.

VIII

PSYCHOTHERAPY/ PSYCHOANALYST

Asylum for the Sane

"**P**sychotherapy is an undefined technique applied to unspecific problems—with unpredictable outcomes for which a rigorous training is required," says Raimy.[1] Actually, these days anyone can simply hang out a shingle and call himself/herself a therapist. And people do. Soon, there will be more psychotherapists than patients.

Psychotherapy is a slow-cooking process; there is no microwave equivalent of it. Becoming a psychotherapist is even slower, like growing up. Because "the therapist's personality overrides all techniques,"[2] the maturation of the therapist is of paramount importance. While anyone can be trained in the techniques of psychotherapy, not everyone can be made a therapeutic person.

In psychotherapy, "there are no rules until you break one,"[3] and both patient and therapist will know it when that happens.

✦✦

Can *unintentional psychotherapy* be a new school?

✦✦

Over the encounter therapies are effective when the patient is not sicker than the therapist.

✦✦

Theoretical monogamy is betrayal of one's patient.

✦✦

Patients who were analyzed by the Oedipal theory—Freudian schools—should be recalled. They are making pre-Oedipal slips.

✦✦

Only within the context of the collective unconscious (e.g., myths) does the personal unconscious make sense.

✦✦

Hollowing dysphoria: One of the most common, and least recognized, psychopathological states.

❧❧

"Addiction is not satisfied by its object,"[4] nor by its substitute.

❧❧

Chronically anxious people are on fear-fulfillment missions.

❧❧

What makes a good patient? One who loves the truth of the therapist.

❧❧

Tears over the past freeze a person, not unlike Lot's wife who turned into a pillar of salt.

❧❧

Most of the earliest childhood traumas are *time-released*, mainly manifesting in late adolescence.

❧❧

Every choice made to stabilize one's self is destabilizing because choices are reversible.

❧❧

The *innocence complex* is the easiest complex from which to recover.

+✢+ +✢+

"Every teacher becomes a bore eventually."[5] Perhaps that is why all behavioral therapies are short-term therapies.

+✢+ +✢+

Psychoanalytical literature is essentially a chain of *conscious associations* from Freud to the present.

+✢+ +✢+

"Every therapy is a relative failure,"[6] but somehow every therapist seems to be an absolute success.

+✢+ +✢+

Psychotherapy is an interpersonal meditation.

+✢+ +✢+

A therapeutic alliance is a technique; what patients really need is a therapeutic union.

+✢+ +✢+

Dogma eat dogma forces a counter-transferential template onto the patient.

+✢+ +✢+

A therapy-soaked life forfeits life itself.

✛✛

Psychotherapy is not so much a profession as a way of being, a soulful and spiritual existence.

✛✛

Psychological theories tend to border on the "illusion of profundity."[7]

✛✛

Psychotherapy is most effective in its iatrogenic disorder.

✛✛

How to roll a string of beads? Don't push, gently pull. A fitting metaphor for moving people.

✛✛

Psychotherapeutic theory: Just Say "No"!

✛✛

The secret of most successful therapeutic relationships is intersubjective synchronicity.

✛✛

Therapist's interventions are "contextualized manifestation of his/her personality."[8] That is why the training of the therapist has a limited value.

+≈+ +≈+

Most patients don't need resolution of some psychological conflicts as much as they need acquisition of a psychological structure.

+≈+ +≈+

Psychoanalysis is an indifferent relationship within an impersonal framework.

+≈+ +≈+

The first psychological task of every person is to establish a self-congruence.

+≈+ +≈+

In psychological growth, there is no end product.

+≈+ +≈+

"The therapist and the patient are each other's fate."[9]

+≈+ +≈+

Analyst clarifications are like *obscurum per obscurius*.

+≈+ +≈+

People change at different rates and in different ways.

+≈+ +≈+

A good patient tries to fit the therapist's theoretical frame.

~+~+

"The process of psychotherapy involves oscillations in small increments between 'getting worse' and 'getting better.'" [10]

~+~+

Each therapist and patient pair has its own timetable for intersubjective resonant healing.

~+~+

Both therapist and patient suffer from the same universal symptom of aloneness, i.e., the need to return to an original undifferentiated state.

~+~+

Every therapy is a play, some good, some bad.

~+~+

Successful psychoanalyses begins with the induction of an artificial illness—transference neuroses.

~+~+

Emotional dialectic: Therapist and patient find themselves in each other.

+≻+ +≻+

The patient finds out what the therapist knows, which is what the patient has always known: no one is himself.

+≻+ +≻+

The ear is no breast.

+≻+ +≻+

Therapeutic misalliance is the ultimate *status descendi*.

+≻+ +≻+

The affective tone of interpretation mutes the critical meaning of messages.

+≻+ +≻+

Cognitive therapy replaced the empathic maternal face of psychodynamic therapy with paternal scorn.

+≻+ +≻+

As with the death of Mark Twain, the demise of psychotherapy is overexaggerated. As long as there is living, dying, being, becoming, and money, there will be psychotherapy.

+≻+ +≻+

What falsifies normal memory? Our wishes and fears.

+∼+ +∼+

Diagnosis is a concluding form of objectification.

+∼+ +∼+

"Psychotherapy is not a field for spectacular successes,"[11] nor is any other field.

+∼+ +∼+

The practice of psychotherapy may make one a better therapist, but not necessarily a better person.

+∼+ +∼+

"Psychotherapy is [not] . . . where the privileged devote themselves to the expensive, selfish, and impotent cultivation of subjectivity."[12] That is the life of the privileged.

+∼+ +∼+

À la Robert Frost on poetry, if I am pressed to reply to the question of "what is psychotherapy," I would say psychotherapy is what a psychotherapist does.

+∼+ +∼+

A psychotherapist who perpetuates a transferential bond rides on the patient's neuroses.

↞↠↞↠

There are punishing alter-superego therapists, reasoning alter-ego therapists, and enabling alter-id therapists.

↞↠↞↠

Generic therapists (psychodynamic, cognitive, dyadic) are technicians; *brand name* therapists are *healers*.

↞↠↞↠

À la Isaac Bashevis Singer on literature, when I am asked to which school of psychotherapy I belong, I am tempted to say modestly that only small fish swim in schools.

↞↠↞↠

Only a healthy therapist can offer him or herself as a substitute psychological structure.

↞↠↞↠

Wounded healers are the most empathic therapists, but not necessarily the most effective.

↞↠↞↠

"The professional ethical tranquility of the therapist primarily depends on his ability to live with chronic mild disillusionment."

❧ ❧

The therapist's only task is to grasp the raw data of experience, for the preconceptual bars provide false security and real limitations.

❧ ❧

The therapist must be surprised by nothing and be surprised by everything.

❧ ❧

At one time or another, the therapist unconsciously allies with the patient to an extreme extent, even colluding with the patient against others—a virtue of his fault.

❧ ❧

"If you ever recognize the patient,"[13] you may have found a validation of your theory. You may also have already lost the patient.

❧ ❧

The therapist becomes the *therapist* only in the relationship to his patients.

❧ ❧

The more often the psychotherapist sees patients, the more likely that he'll expand his *interactive repertoire*.

Therapists are teachers of sanity, even though they themselves may not be so sane.

The quality of a psychotherapist is strongly correlated
with his or her worth as a person.

A therapist's ear should never be innocent.

The interpretations of one therapist may be no better than
many other therapists, but the length of the silences after
an interpretation—ah, that is where the art of therapy
resides.

Patients come to treatment in search of a substitute object,
if not a substitute self.

The therapist who "completely understands the patient"[14]
has stopped listening.

❧❧

Id-therapists are "psycho-plagiarists."

❧❧

Some people apply to the mental health professions *for the wrong reasons*. Hopefully they evolve into the right ones.

❧❧

When the therapist becomes a therapist, the patient arrives.

❧❧

Dogmatic relativism is the source of therapeutic atheism.

❧❧

Theories of psychotherapy should anchor, not drown, the therapist.

❧❧

By heightening or lowering arousal, the therapist enters the patient's world.

❧❧

Good moments and sudden insights may deceive the patient and derail the therapist.

+~+ +~+

Like a poet, a psychotherapist who is utterly clear is a trifle glaring.

+~+ +~+

Transferential fitness, is the source of long-lasting therapies.

+~+ +~+

The *last therapist* will dwell uncomfortably at a distance from the primacy of theory.

+~+ +~+

Therapists are not immune from the afflictions of their patients.

+~+ +~+

A therapist at best can get the patient to the level of personal growth that he himself personally has reached.

NOTES

1. Raimy, Victor, PhD., ed. 1950. *Training in Clinical Psychology*. Englewood Cliffs, N.J.: Prentice-Hall, p. 93.

2. Chessick, Richard, M.D., personal communication.

3. Hillman, James, PhD., personal communication.

4. Zukav, Gary, personal communication.

5. Beck, Aaron T., M.D., personal communication.

6. May, Rollo, PhD., personal communication.

7. Langs, Robert, M.D., personal communication.

8. Friedman, Lawrence, M.D. 1988. *Anatomy of Psychotherapy*. Hillsdale, N.J.: The Analytic Press, Hove & London.

9. Peck, M. Scott, M.D., personal communication.

10. Havens, Leston, M.D., personal communication.

11. Benson, Herbert, M.D., personal communication.

12. Unger, Roberto Mangabeira. 1984. *Passion: An Essay on Personality*. New York: Free Press, Collier MacMillan Publishers.

13. Coleman, Jules, PhD., personal communication.

14. Arlow, Jacob, M.D., personal communication.

IX

GOD/RELIGION

To Believe the Unbelievable

Since the beginning of time, there have been religions and gods. They served as laws of conduct for each specific tribe. Unbelievers were simply asocial in the community. Otherwise there were no conflicts within the social structure, because religion and its gods were part of each culture. This construct worked until isolated tribes began to cross their geographic boundaries and encountered other gods. Since then, the battles of "my god is better (bigger) than yours" have been raging with increasing determination.

Meanwhile, the original purpose of god and religion seems to have been forgotten. Religion is an external communion, intended to bind people together, not to turn people against others. God is ideal. We are supposed to emulate God's principles—to be loving, forgiving, truthful, compassionate people. That is to be "godly" with a small "g."

If we all share the same "Divine womb," stop kicking.

✦ ✦

All religions preach love and hate each other.

✦ ✦

"The best evidence of God's existence is his absence."[1]

✦ ✦

Impending dangers make one faithful.

✦ ✦

I think, I feel, I believe, and I act, and therefore I am.

✦ ✦

There is north because there is south; there is plus because there is minus; there is good because there is bad; and there is God because there is man.

✦ ✦

Ritualism is benign obsessive-compulsive behavior.

✦ ✦

Religion provides continuity of the past, the present, and the eternal future, however illusionary.

+≈+ +≈+

If you give children more than one option of religion, they may fall faithless between the cracks of faith.

+≈+ +≈+

Only rituals enacted within a specific religious context have spiritual footings.

+≈+ +≈+

Without religion, a man is homeless; if he builds his own home with his own philosophy, he will live in it alone.

+≈+ +≈+

The ultimate purpose of sinning is not to seek redemption but to arrive *at a stage as not to need to sin.*

+≈+ +≈+

"Centering" requires "knitting yourself"[2] into your family, your community, and your spiritual home.

+≈+ +≈+

Spiritual descent impregnates the soul.

+≈+ +≈+

Sinning fertilizes the spirit.

+≈+ +≈+

Traditional religions have outstripped their conceptual bases; so has secular spirituality.

+≈+ +≈+

Eventually, from all that you love and hate, you must part.

+≈+ +≈+

You might either extinguish your desire, as in Taoism, or transmute it to love, as in Christianity, but don't let it idle. It will get you into trouble.

+≈+ +≈+

Yoga in Sanskrit means "unite"—uniting your mind and body, with the universe. If you could just unite your mind with your body, you are already a Yogi.

+≈+ +≈+

All religions say essentially the same thing: Do this and be good and then know this and be godly.

+≈+ +≈+

Knowledge of God is divine ignorance.

+≈+ +≈+

The love of sect is communal self-love.

No secular war wins in fighting a religious one.

Enthusiasm means having God within; it should also carry you to anywhere God is without.

One cannot articulate the concept of God without damage to religions.

Against his better judgment, man has an overwhelming need to settle for a story that promises immortality.

Faith is a paradigm by which man can find meaning in his life.

The turning of one's mind exclusively into God loses both.

Reality is incomplete, if viewed from secular point of view, and it is incoherent, if viewed from religious point of view.

✦✧✦

In his private isolation, every man recognizes his nothingness.

✦✧✦

The atheist who preaches nihilism is a closet believer.

✦✧✦

A belief is true because it is useful.

✦✧✦

Conscience is the prosecutor, the judge, and the victim; the defense never rests.

✦✧✦

God descended and impregnated a woman; man ascended and remained a virgin.

✦✧✦

If everything were explainable by our minds, there would be no need for God.

✦✧✦

Religious fanatics are the real atheists, for they deny the purpose of God.

✛✛✛✛

Conscience has its own punishment: guilt.

✛✛✛✛

Tertullian's rule *I believe it because it is absurd*, applies not only to faith.

✛✛✛✛

Every man believes his own religion as real and tolerable, but finds all other religions unbelievable, counterfeit, and intolerable.

✛✛✛✛

Belong to a sect of one; it'll protect you against any religious epidemics.

✛✛✛✛

Belonging is outer communion.

✛✛✛✛

Sooner or later, all archaic reactions exhaust themselves in the field of substitution.

✛✛✛✛

Moses was a threatening father; Jesus was a loving mother. Sooner or later we've got to leave home.

†◌+◌†

God is everywhere, and nowhere. Just make sure you know where you are.

†◌+◌†

Today's "Mc-religions" consist of the intellectual debris left from the original misconception.

†◌+◌†

All three Abrahamic texts deliver advice, prohibition, love or threats, without any sense of humor.

†◌+◌†

"In the beginning there was the word"; at the end, the period.

NOTES

1. A Tertullian saying.
2. Dyer, Wayne, PhD., personal communication.

X

SOUL/SPIRITUALITY
Cultivating Other People's Gardens

Voltaire[1] attributes happiness to "cultivating one's own garden." In fact, happiness is cultivating other people's gardens: being soulful and spiritual.

Soul and Spirit fire separately: Soul pulls you down to earth—to love others, work, and belonging; Spirit pulls you up—to believe in the sacred, in unity, and in transformation. In tandem they deliver *the thing* that everyone is yearning for—Serenity.

Novelist and priest André Malraux[2] sums up what he learned about humans in his decades of service: "There is no saintly person." Well, that is because there are so few grown-ups. The "path to sainthood goes through adulthood," says M. Scott Peck.[3] A happy adult is one who lives in joyful serenity—a psychological state anchored in a soulful and spiritual existence, real or illusionary.

One can only wobble against the background of stillness.

†✧†✧†

Before Adam and Eve, there was a garden.

†✧†✧†

Go to joyful places: to witty, pleasant, genuine and affectionate ones.

†✧†✧†

Outer pollution blackens your lungs; *inner pollution* blackens your soul.

†✧†✧†

"Puzzlement precedes either enlightenment or delusion."[4]

†✧†✧†

Every ending has its own beginning.

†✧†✧†

You should not rest on your soulful laurels; you must also strive for spirituality.

†✧†✧†

For meditation to be truly meditative, it must be joyful.

❦❦

You cannot decide to restructure yourself; the self is cultivated in a *felt life*.

❦❦

Spirituality doesn't promote fast growth, as it will have
weak roots and be easily torn up.

❦❦

A god-like existence is believing in "the predicate theol-
ogy"[5]: love is god, truth is god, compassion is god . . . .

❦❦

Humans are homogenous creatures in essence, though not
in form.

❦❦

Our body is a universal body; our mind is a universal mind.

❦❦

The state of nondifferentiation from the universe is living
everywhere and in everything, and forever.

❦❦

Soulfulness cannot be sought, or found, or even lost.

✦✦✦

"No seed ever sees its flower."[6] Nature provides the meaning of life: assuring spiritual continuity.

✦✦✦

There is no 'I'; there is no here; there is no now. Serenity is a state of being undifferentiated from time and place and other beings.

✦✦✦

Enlightenment is the absence of a self-serving existence.

✦✦✦

For the spiritual, the *not knowing* is evolving.

✦✦✦

Savor unacceptable wishes and "spit them out like a wine taster."[7]

✦✦✦

There are only degrees of being.

✦✦✦

Serenity is inner and outer stillness.

۰ぐ۰ぐ

Spiritual wellness: There is no royal road to it, simply a sacred one.

۰ぐ۰ぐ

If you believe in *peace, love, understanding*, you don't need to claim divinity; you are divine.

۰ぐ۰ぐ

The enlightened man is under-determined.

۰ぐ۰ぐ

The enlightened man maintains a certain free margin, and sense of curiosity and credulity. He doesn't presume to have arrived, has no claims, or piety: he is a puzzled perpetual learner.

۰ぐ۰ぐ

Take the better; the best seldom comes.

۰ぐ۰ぐ

The truth is the appropriation of compassionate resonance.

۰ぐ۰ぐ

Change occurs by understanding the way of sameness.

+~+ +~+

Do not aim at the center: life is a moving target.

+~+ +~+

If you don't hear the space between sounds, you are not listening.

+~+ +~+

There is no behavior that makes no sense, or that makes sense. There are no neurotics, and there are no normals. There are only degrees of equanimity in view of the human dilemma.

+~+ +~+

We are all seeking.

+~+ +~+

Happiness is formless and discontinuous. You couldn't know, even if you knew.

+~+ +~+

"Kneel at the feet of nature"[8] and listen; it's the only sermon you need.

✦✦ ✦✦

An intrapsychic dialogue is being both subject and object of one's thoughts and feelings, culminating in transcendental silence: *The Amongst Itness.*

✦✦ ✦✦

Being is not a passive, contemplative life, but an active and rigorous one.

✦✦ ✦✦

Only redemptive relationships are transformative. This redemption is not geared toward sins, but to the redemption from one's mind. There is no blame, no fault, no punishment, no forgiveness. It is the rescue of self from the self.

✦✦ ✦✦

While the spiritual sustains the knowledge that each individual has an entirely separate existence, she seeks to confirm the sacred evidence of oneness.

✦✦ ✦✦

Emancipation from the confinement of human entanglements and deliverance from the imprisonment of our minds expand the self and evoke harmony with one's self and the universe.

✦✦✦✦

Spirituality is not normative, but transformative; it extracts meaning out of meaningless.

✦✦✦✦

The soulful never draw emotional blood.

✦✦✦✦

The healer melts down the *hard facts*.

✦✦✦✦

Authentic communication is neither verbal nor silent; it is an irreducible communion.

✦✦✦✦

There is no meaning of life; there could be meaning for your life—the one that you bring to it.

✦✦✦✦

Spiritual union is knowingly "accepting the other's counterfeit coin."[9]

✦✦✦✦

One doesn't find happiness by pursuing it; happiness is a by-product of pursuing a purposeful life. Happiness is a path, not a destination.

⁺∿⁺∿⁺

When there is no cake, you can eat it and still have it.

⁺∿⁺∿⁺

Sisyphus was a happy man because he was forever busy.

⁺∿⁺∿⁺

Only wise sayings delivered in kindness are useful.

⁺∿⁺∿⁺

We are blindsided by our own eyes.

⁺∿⁺∿⁺

Information comes and goes; knowledge lingers, but wisdom sediments.

⁺∿⁺∿⁺

You can learn the world by information, by knowledge, by experience, or know it by intuition.

⁺∿⁺∿⁺

Cunning and innocence share the same common well: the human mind.

❧❧

Charity as well as all other benevolences, such as love, affection, kindness, and compassion, might begin at home, but it must not be confined there.

❧❧

Don't point the way to others unless you have walked the path and arrived at the destination.

❧❧

Self-doubt is the beginning and end of wisdom.

❧❧

If someone gives you nothing, take it.

❧❧

Deserve more, desire less.

❧❧

Your future lot is not a preordained destiny, but rather mostly decreed by your past.

❧❧

Frame your wit in dullness.

Having a good intention is not enough: you must do good.

Forgive yourself, but do not ever forget what you forgave yourself for.

This moment is the only time.

Before scaling to heaven, first ascend on earth.

Here it was, here it is, here it'll not be.

Truth may be useful, wit may be amusing; when combined, they are neither useful nor amusing.

Zeal and wit are fit only for the wise.

Spiritual transcendence requires that you have to have something to transcend—adulthood.

+✦+ +✦+

You can get wet quickly running in the rain—a quick course in life—or little by little strolling in a fog—distillation of your experiences.

+✦+ +✦+

All seekings are transitional; there is no *terra firma* in life.

+✦+ +✦+

Felt cognition: insight more caught than thought.

+✦+ +✦+

Neither joy nor suffering by itself is noble nor necessary for soul making and character building; it is to what use you put either.

+✦+ +✦+

The ultimate love is "a love with no object."[10]

+✦+ +✦+

The ultimate attunement is a resonance with the intransmissible.

+✦+ +✦+

There is no present (i.e., an indivisible point), just the past and the future.

+❧+ +❧+

We all share a *common well*; do not poison it.

Notes

1. Voltaire, Francois-Marie Arouet de. 1759. *Candide*, Chapter 30.

2. Malraux, André. 1968. *Anti-memoirs*, trans. Terence Kilmartin. New York: Holt, Rinehart, and Winston, p. 1.

3. Peck, M. Scott, M.D. 1993. *Further Along the Road Less Traveled: The Unending Journey toward Spiritual Growth*. New York: Touchstone, p. 159.

4. Chopra, Deepak, M.D., personal communication.

5. Kushner, Harold, Rabbi, personal communication.

6. A Buddhist saying.

7. Kernberg, Otto, M.D., personal communication.

8. A Zen saying.

9. Moore, Thomas, PhD., personal communication.

10. Chopra, Deepak, M.D., personal communication.

· XI ·

STRESS/WELLNESS
Self-Ministered Sufferings

M ost of our stresses are self-induced—by not being satisfied with what we have. This may be exactly the opposite of what the current culture celebrates: ambition, hard drive, constant expectations of rewards and promotions.

Because there is no end to what we may want, we are chronically stressed. This stress constantly pumps harsh and edgy adrenaline and cortisol into the body, requiring ever increasing amounts of tranquilizers and sleeping pills to calm it down. Conversely, wellness swims with softer and warmer innate hormones and neurotransmitters—endorphins and serotonin.

Both stress and wellness are generated by the mind and expedited by the brain. That is what is meant by *it is all in your head*—mostly.

CHAPTER XI

Psychological mutilation is not quantifiable.

＋∾＋∾＋

One's psychological trauma is a chronic process, and rarely a discrete event.

＋∾＋∾＋

Form follows failure: Medicine makes different overwrought, overargued claims, then recants them with the same conviction, only to reclaim them again.

＋∾＋∾＋

Contentment comes from *wishing for what you already have*. If you wish for what you don't have, you'll be perennially discontent.

＋∾＋∾＋

Thoughts of suicide may have saved many lives, but urging depressed people to think of suicide is murder.

＋∾＋∾＋

Both *intra* and *extrasensory perceptions* are just perceptions, not immune from false positives and negatives.

＋∾＋∾＋

Tame your anxiety but not your fears.

+⌇+ +⌇+

If a lie defines a person's agenda, that person cannot negate the lie without negating his or her own self.

+⌇+ +⌇+

Chronic anxiety and dysphoria ride on insomnia, making a person less attractive.

+⌇+ +⌇+

Stress is the by-product of powerlessness, whatever its nature, and whether it is real or imagined.

+⌇+ +⌇+

All achievements do not alter *the neurotic core of a person.*

+⌇+ +⌇+

Slogans are enthusiastic expressions of self-doubt.

+⌇+ +⌇+

Positive events are as stressful as the negative ones: finishing college, getting married, buying a new house, having a child, being promoted, etc.

+⌇+ +⌇+

Mockery is witless dismissal by the scared.

✦✦ ✦✦

The extraordinariness of ego-ideals and id-ideals are anti-dotes against our common ordinariness.

✦✦ ✦✦

Chronic preoccupation with possessions leads to pervasive fatigue.

✦✦ ✦✦

All animals are simply aware; humans are aware of their awareness.

✦✦ ✦✦

Psychological longevity is dependent on psychological maintenance.

✦✦ ✦✦

"Anger is directed towards others; rage is towards the self."[1]

✦✦ ✦✦

Antisocial behavior is not quantifiable.

✦✦ ✦✦

Obesity is contagious.

✦✦✦✦

Physical and psychological stresses are the deferred punishment of living a long life.

✦✦✦✦

Being bored is a form of dysphoria; being boring is a grievous offense.

✦✦✦✦

If you are unable to tell clearly what is your psychological problem, someone will give a diagnosis.

✦✦✦✦

Psychological and physical illness are messages from within, urging us to reframe our lives.

✦✦✦✦

The past was misunderstood, the present is misunderstanding; the future is predicted in terms of the past and the present.

✦✦✦✦

Anxious people fear any change, especially if it is for the better.

✦✦

Your disappointment in life correlates with what you are capable of wanting.

✦✦

Everyone needs a practical philosophy that does not pontificate on infinity, but systematically reflects upon how to live best—given the circumstances.

✦✦

All emotions are lost in translation.

✦✦

Moral indignation is an indulgence in justifying sadism.

✦✦

Amusements postpone unhappiness.

✦✦

Too many alternatives are paralyzing.

✦✦

Tears and fears permanently imprint memories.

✦✦

Draw a small circle around yourself and step out.

❧❦❧

Don't keep going over the past, reimprinting old material, unless it is pleasant.

❧❦❧

Every restrained passion converts to wisdom; every inflamed passion to regrets.

❧❦❧

The distance between occasional and often defines addiction.

❧❦❧

Even beggars are territorial.

❧❦❧

The one who always rings the bell will suffer from tinnitus.

❧❦❧

Don't carry your head over your height; you'll get hit.

❧❦❧

Who is too anxious to please, displeases.

❧❦❧

Unlike birds, build on your last year's nest.

᚛᚛᚛᚛

Practice old truths, not old errors.

᚛᚛᚛᚛

If you are discontent in winter, you may have seasonal depression; but if you are always in the winter of your discontent, you are just a fickle human.

᚛᚛᚛᚛

Disgrace is a recurrent disease; one never fully recovers from it.

᚛᚛᚛᚛

Indulge in *enoughs*.

᚛᚛᚛᚛

In all its circularities, the time remains linear.

᚛᚛᚛᚛

The truth is felt more than known.

᚛᚛᚛᚛

The guiltless fear the Law; the guilty dread the nights.

A sense of vulnerability is the source of an excessive use of power.

The mind cannot reflect upon itself, never mind the stressed mind.

Anxiety and depression are common fuels for intellectual and artistic creativity for a very small minority. The rest are simply made miserable by them.

The second half of a man's life is made up of nothing but doubts about everything he learned during the first half.

Activities that emanate from without (e.g., listening to music, watching sports, reading) are entertainment; activities emanating from within (e.g., playing a sport or an instrument, writing) are regenerative.

Indulging into the agony of grief is baiting the pleasure of melancholy.

+<>+ +<>+

Good health is never felt, but ill health is ever present in mind.

+<>+ +<>+

Serenity is to have nothing to repent in life.

+<>+ +<>+

Reflect before you act. The reverse sequence comes with heavy self-punishment.

+<>+ +<>+

The real strength of a person shows at the breaking point.

+<>+ +<>+

Whenever you think of something wrong in your life, make a habit of finding what is right in it.

+<>+ +<>+

Any pleasure that borders satiety treads upon grief.

+<>+ +<>+

Depression is an ever present master of all illnesses.

+<>+ +<>+

Passion is the only cure for the tedium of existence.

+~+ +~+

Punishment is included in the sin. So do not seek further retribution.

+~+ +~+

Hate is everlasting self-punishment.

+~+ +~+

The meaning of life comes from the distillation of one's experiences.

+~+ +~+

It is the greatest felicity to be born, regardless of what kind of spoon is in your mouth. Just take it out.

+~+ +~+

If you kick the dust, some will get into your eyes.

+~+ +~+

You are imprisoned in your body, but you can improve on the accommodations.

+~+ +~+

"Don't scrape the bottom of anything solid."[2]

❧❧

Doing injustice to someone carries its own punishment: guilt for a good man; fear for the rest.

❧❧

Hope feeds on fear.

❧❧

Neither vice nor virtue is hereditary; you can take credit for either all by yourself.

❧❧

Living is contending with adversities, with occasional probational relief.

❧❧

Wellness means psychological, physical and financial fitness.

❧❧

Wisely trust, unless you are already paranoid.

❧❧

Don't abuse the present by extolling your past.

+◌+ +◌+

You don't have to love or hate money, just remain friendly with it.

+◌+ +◌+

Sometimes you should "quit while you are behind."[3]

+◌+ +◌+

If you run a race of your own, you can't lose.

+◌+ +◌+

Laugh a lot, cry and weep; live a felt life.

NOTES

1. Kernberg, Otto, M.D., personal communication.

2. Nixon, Richard M., personal communication.

3. Osman Effendi, the last Prince Héritier of the Ottoman Empire, personal communication.

· XII ·
AGING/DEATH
From Here to Nowhere

I n ancient Greece a depressed aging person was called *a child of Saturn*—someone who is suffering from the loss of his or her youthfulness.

Well, that loss is everyone's fate for having lived a long life. But only those who carry a dignified *halo of melancholy* similar to the ring of Saturn age and die gracefully.

Aging has the potential to give a certain weight and density to our presence, coalescing life experiences into a meaningful philosophy that enables us *to come to terms* with our ending. Of course, if we never came to terms with our beginning, we may not want to come to terms with our ending either.

The indescribable dread of *no longer being* is one reason that prevents our living out this most extraordinary experience of our life: dying. The other reason: having forfeited life. Without having lived in *everythingness*, it is difficult to accept dissolution to *nothingness*. However, it will happen—the earth is our witness.

The old suffer every new invention.

✦✦✦✦

If you don't die at the height of your obituary, skip the memorial.

✦✦✦✦

Dysphoria about getting older offers density to one's character.

✦✦✦✦

The more you live your life to the fullest, the less you'll fear death.

✦✦✦✦

If you don't come to terms with your old regrets, a chronic anger may seize you and begin to gnaw on your bones.

✦✦✦✦

You cannot imagine your absence, unless you have been and are present.

✦✦✦✦

We all bear the seed of self-destruction.

❧❧

The leak may not be where the drip is, but the house will still flood.

❧❧

A good death cannot be improvised at the last minute. Have a few full dress rehearsals while you are young and healthy.

❧❧

If a drop of the sea doesn't suffice to convince you that it is salty, drowning in it might.

❧❧

Eliminating awareness lowers anxiety.

❧❧

Time is too slow a killer.

❧❧

There is only a monologue with death.

❧❧

One who tastes death savors life.

✦✦ ✦✦

"One dies the way one has lived,"[1] so drink deep from the well.

✦✦ ✦✦

Serious illness transforms a person; it enables the person to be finally himself.

✦✦ ✦✦

The indignity of old age is best coped by lowering of the flag.

✦✦ ✦✦

Grow young by learning something new every day.

✦✦ ✦✦

Emotions are fuels, some generative, some toxic.

✦✦ ✦✦

Fear of death comes from not having lived.

✦✦ ✦✦

The ending of one's life tends to be untidy, unless you let someone else do it for you.

❦❦❦

Obviously *in the long run we are all dead*. But focus on the short run: we are all alive.

❦❦❦

In death-related conversations, the essence of *death* seems always to escape.

❦❦❦

Only primordial dissolution—nothingness—is everything.

❦❦❦

When one has lost all hope about the future, one begins to write an autobiography.

❦❦❦

No one believes he is old until he meets friends he has not seen in a long time.

❦❦❦

Once you come to terms with your death, you'll be free to live the present fully.

❦❦❦

At birth and death, all men are equal, but in between the same truth cannot be held self-evident.

+~+ +~+

You had cried when you were born. Live a life to assure that someone cries when you die.

+~+ +~+

Reactions to *the funnies* through the ages: hardy laughter, chuckling, gentle smile, scorn.

+~+ +~+

Progression of forgetfulness in an aging mind: last names, first names, names of objects, predicates, verbs, and finally the subject—the self.

+~+ +~+

Progression of human emotions: joy, delight, wonderment, euphoria, curiosity, anxiety, passion, envy, jealousy, irritability, anger, rage, dysphoria, regrets, depression, indifference, confusion.

+~+ +~+

In his old age Freud added the death instinct (Thanatos) to his two other instincts: sex and aggression. That is the phase of one's life in which the other two instincts become irrelevant.

✦✦✦✦

Some people don't just get old, they get buried alive in their *oldness*.

✦✦✦✦

The mind cannot tolerate the open-ended disorder of not knowing.

✦✦✦✦

Some medicines given to terminal patients may increase their lives by a year. But that year is a business of daily torture.

✦✦✦✦

We do not necessarily grow gentler or better as we get older; we grow more like ourselves.

✦✦✦✦

You can limp along with, or dance out of time.

✦✦✦✦

The Earth is everyone's final home.

✦✦✦✦

The fear of death is misplaced; it is dying that deserves attention.

✧✧ ✧✧

"Anatomy is destiny," Freud[2] rewords Napoleon's famous statement, but so is physiology, biology and chemistry.

✧✧ ✧✧

The more you have to lose, the more you'll be afraid of dying.

✧✧ ✧✧

We are all citizens of time.

✧✧ ✧✧

To have truly lived life means to be fully aware and in control of one's dying.

✧✧ ✧✧

"Eternity is like an infinite mode of transient moments."[3]

✧✧ ✧✧

Life is intermission between two extraordinary events: birth and death.

✧✧ ✧✧

Death is transformation from an organic state to an inorganic one. A small consolation prize.

✦✧✦✧

Only those who surpass their successors live for eternity.

✦✧✦✧

The grave: the ultimate privacy, even from one's self.

✦✧✦✧

If you have one foot in the grave, make sure that the other is not in the hospital.

✦✧✦✧

Make every funeral you attend yours; your own funeral is not yours.

✦✧✦✧

You'll be missed, temporarily.

NOTES

1. Frank, Jerome, M.D., personal communication.

2. Freud, Sigmund. *The Standard Edition of the Complete Psychological Works of Sigmund Freud, Vol. xi*, ed. James Strachey, 1957.

3. Campbell, Joseph, personal communication.

About the Author

T. Byram Karasu, M.D., is the Silverman Professor and University Chairman of the Department of Psychiatry and Behavioral Sciences at Albert Einstein College of Medicine/Montefiore Medical Center, and the editor-in-chief of the *American Journal of Psychotherapy*. Dr. Karasu chaired the American Psychiatric Association's Commission on Psychiatric Therapies, which produced a critical review of all practiced psychological therapies in the United States. He is the author or editor of nineteen books, including two novels, *Of God and Madness* and *Gotham Chronicles: The Culture of Sociopathy*; a book of poetry, *Rags of My Soul*; and two best sellers, *The Art of Serenity* and *The Spirit of Happiness*. Dr. Karasu is a scholar, renowned clinician, teacher, and lecturer, and the recipient of numerous awards. He lives in New York City.